DATE DUE

CARS

Franklin Watts
95 Madison Avenue
New York, NY 10016

Library of Congress Cataloging-in-Publication Data

Richardson, Joy.
  Cars / Joy Richardson
     p. cm. – (Picture science)
  Includes index.
  ISBN 0-531-14325-2
  1. Automobiles – Juvenile literature. [1. Automobiles.]
I. Title. II. Series: Richardson, Joy. Picture science.
TL206.R53   1994   93-42179
629.2–dc20   CIP AC

10 9 8 7 6 5 4 3 2 1

Editor: Belinda Weber
Designer: Janet Watson
Picture researcher: Sarah Moule
Illustrators: Robert and Rhoda Burns

Photographs: Eye Ubiquitous © Steve Brock 6; Ford 28;
Quadrant 21; Robert Harding Picture Library 18; Tony Stone
Worldwide 24, © Donald Johnston cover; © Ken Biggs 23;
Transport Research Laboratory 16; Zefa title page, 9, 11, 12,15, 26.

Printed in Malaysia

PICTURE SCIENCE

CARS

Joy Richardson

FRANKLIN WATTS

New York • Chicago • London • Toronto • Sydney

Cars everywhere

Just over one hundred years ago,
the first horseless carriages
bumped and sputtered
along the roads.

These cars used engine power
instead of horse power.
At first they were slow and
noisy and broke down often.

No one could have guessed
how popular they would become.

Today there are billions
of cars on the road.

Made by hand

At first cars were built
by hand, one at a time.
They were very expensive
but made to last.

They had shiny brass fittings,
polished wood trim, and
padded leather seats.

They had starting handles
to get them going and hoods
to pull up when it rained.

Car factory

Henry Ford found a new way
of making cars in the United States.

He used a production line.
Each worker did one job as
the car moved through the factory.

Cars could be made more quickly,
which meant more cars could be
made and sold for less money.

Since then, millions of cars
have rolled off production
lines all over the world.
Now many of the jobs
can be done by robots.

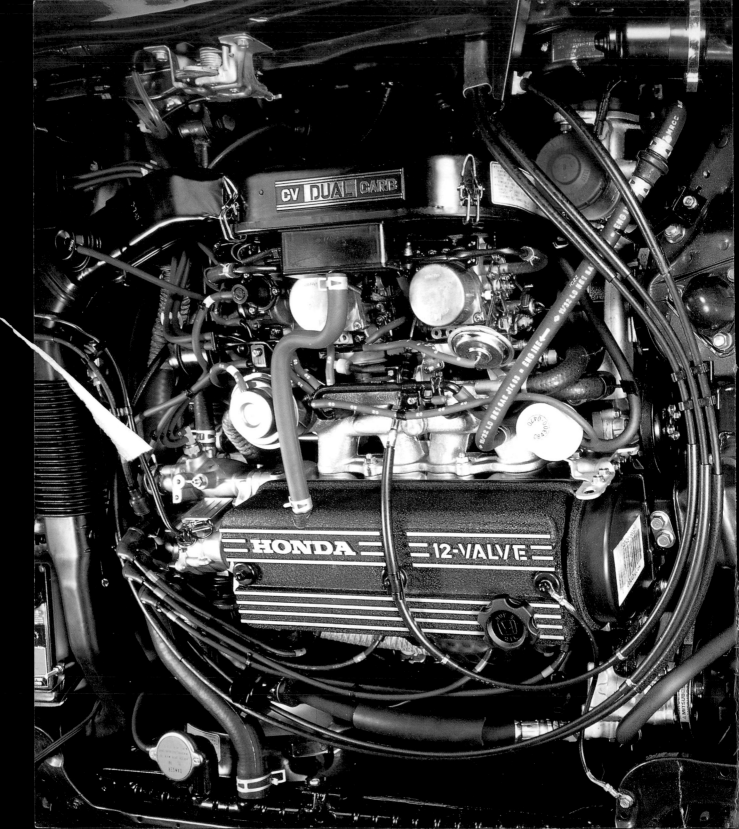

Engine power

Engines are put together and then fitted into the car.

Each engine contains a set of cylinders.

Inside the cylinders, fuel and air catch fire and explode, driving the pistons up and down. This motion turns the rod, which goes through the gearbox and out to wheels.

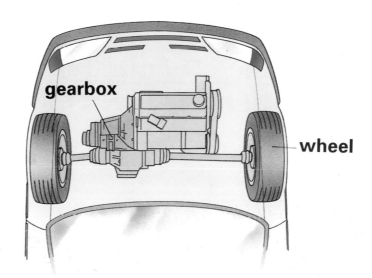

gearbox

wheel

Turning wheels

In most cars, the engine powers the front wheels and the back ones follow along.

Cars made for driving on rough or slippery ground have engines that power all four wheels.

The steering wheel is connected to the front wheels and makes them change direction.

There are brakes on all four wheels to stop them turning.

Tires are shaped to grip the road even when it is wet or icy.

Car body

The car body is put together and then fitted onto the rest of the car.

The body is made from sheets of steel, which are pressed into shape for each panel.

The panels are welded together and coated with many layers of paint to protect them.

The car body is tested for safety. Dummies are used to check what would happen to a person in a crash.

Space inside

Inside the car, the seats
are shaped for comfort.
Safety belts are firmly anchored.
Suspension springs cushion the car
and give passengers a smooth ride.

The inside is carefully planned
to give people room and
leave space for luggage.

Sedan cars have a trunk with a lid.
Hatchbacks have space behind the seats.
Station wagons have plenty of room
in the back.

In control

Cars can be built with the controls on the left or the right, for use in different countries.

Facing the driver's seat are the controls.

The driver works the steering wheel, the gearstick, the handbrake, and switches for lights and wipers.

Foot pressure on the accelerator pedal makes the car go faster and the brake is pressed to slow down and the clutch to change gear.

The driver watches the road in front, looks in the mirrors to see behind the car, and checks dials on the dashboard.

On the outside

Each car has a license plate
on the front or back.
Every car has a different number.

Lights on the outside of the car
give messages to other drivers.

Indicators flash to show
which way the car is turning.

Red lights turn on to
show the car is braking.

At night, bright headlights
shine along the road in front.
Red lights warn cars behind.

Streamlined for speed

Cars are streamlined so that
air flows around them smoothly
without holding them back
and wasting fuel.

New designs for cars are
tested in wind tunnels to
see how well the shape works.

The faster a car goes, the harder the air
pushes against it, and the
more streamlining the car needs.

Sports cars have powerful engines
and are streamlined for high speed.

air flow

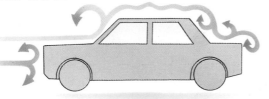

air flow

25

Built to win

Grand Prix racing cars
are the fastest of all.

Every part of the car is
designed for winning races.

The bodies are made of carbon-fibers
that are lighter but stronger than metal.

The tires are wide and smooth
to keep a good grip on the track.

Wings on the front and back are
shaped to make air hold the car
down on the ground.

Over the years, ideas from racing cars
have helped to improve other cars.

Car facts

The first gasoline-powered car
was made in Germany in 1885.

The number of new cars
made each year is now
about forty million.

The cleanest cars are solar-powered.
Sunraycer is the fastest car
running on sunshine.

Index